The Poetry of John Payne

Volume I - Lautrec and The Masque of Shadows

John Payne was born on 23rd August 1842 in Bloomsbury, London.

He began his career in the legal profession but thus was soon put to one side as he began his renowned translations of Boccaccio's Decameron, The Arabian Nights, and then the poets Omar Khayyam, François Villon and Diwan Hafez. Of the latter, who he ranked in the same bracket as Dante and Shakepeare, he said; he takes the "whole sweep of human experience and irradiates all things with his sun-gold and his wisdom"

Later Payne became involved with limited edition publishing, and the Villon Society, which was dedicated to the poems of François Villon who was Frances' best known poet of the middle Ages and unfortunately also a thief and a murderer.

 John Payne died on 11th February, 1916 at the age of 73 in South Kensington, London.

Index of Contents

LAUTREC

The moon comes strangely late to-night,
And yet meseems the dusk has laid
On all its woven hands of shade;
Spent is the tall wan altar-light
And the last vesper-prayer is pray'd.

The last chimes of the vesper bell
Along the sighing wind have died;
And as it were a shadowtide
Rolled upward from the gates of Hell,
The stem gloom surges far and wide.

I lie close shut within my bier;
And yet, despite the graven stone,
I feel the spells the night has strown.
The spells of sorcery and fear.
Unto me through the air sink down:

The many-mingling influences;
The viewless throb of awful mights;
The flutter of the grey-wing'd sprights;
A press of shadowy semblances;
The dreadful things that fly by nights.

I feel the spells of Fate and Fear
That hold the empire of the dark:
Like unseen birds their flight I mark
Athwart the teeming air and hear
The ghosts rush past me, as I hark.

Lo! there the charm fled through the night
That sets the witch's black soul free
To revel over earth and sea,
Whilst the reft corpse lies stark and white:
And still the grave grips hold on me.

Ah! there again the hot thrill swept
Across the dusk brown-breasted air.
I know it: see, the graves gape bare,
Answering; and one by one, upleapt,
The hell-hounds startle from their lair.

A flash as of a dead man's eyes,
Blue as the fires that streak the storm!
And from their dwelling with the worm.
See where the restless spirits rise,
Each like a vapour in man's form.

The signs begin to thicken fast:
A noise of horns, as if there blew
The clarions of all storms that brew
Within the world-womb for the blast
That bids the earth and sea renew:

And to that call the shapes rouse forth
That make night weird with wailing ghosts
Of frightful beasts, whose flame-breathed hosts
East unto West and South to North
Laid waste of old the night's grey coasts;

Until the Christ-god came to bear
Back with his smile the age's gloom,
And withered back into their doom.
They died: yet, wraiths of what they were,
Still in the night they cheat the tomb

And wander over hill and dale.
An awful host, invisible:
But he, who &res by wood and dell,
Hears their wings rustle and their wail
Shrills through him like a wind of hell.

I know them all, ghost, witch and beast;
I hear them hurtle through the gloom;
The glad ghosts scatter from their room;
The ghouls fare forth unto the feast:
Still I lie box within the tomb.

For lo! the Queen of my desire,—
The dreadful Lady of the Night,
That fills my veins with wine of light,
Sacring me with her cold white fire,—
Sleeps yet cloud-hidden from my sight

And here I lie, wrapt in my shroud,
Moveless and cold upon the bier;
And all my rage of wish and fear
Unto the hush I cry aloud,
In tones that only sprites may hear.

And in the fever of my mood,
The passion of the days of yore
Swims like a mist of flame before
My haggard eyes,—a mist of blood,
A meteor-play of tears and gore.

And one white face, mark'd out in lines
And silver characters of fire.
Flames like a phantom of desire
Against my sight; and through the pines
The night-wind, screaming nigh and nigher.

Is as a well remember'd voice,
That once to me was honey-sweet
As that the white soul waits to greet.
When heaven's sight bids the eye rejoice,
Opening upon the golden street.

Ay, once that visage was to me
As Christ's face seen upon the rim
Of heaven, betwixt the cherubim;
That voice was as the melody
Of angels calling, through the dim

Hush'd heart of Death, to him who lies
And waits the coming of the feet
Of that white angel stem and sweet,
That gives the keys of Paradise
Or opens up Hell's sulphur-seat.

There was great love betwixt us twain:
The memory of the time we kiss'd
In passionate innocence, nor wist
Of any harm, will never wane,
Maugre this bloody moonshot mist.

Despite this trance of tears and blood.
Remember it for aye shall I;
And the warm lovelight in his eye.
When for my answering kiss he sued,
Will haunt my curst eternity.

Yea, though the fathomless abyss
Of doom lie gaped our souls between.
His soul, that walks in Heaven's sheen,
Shall burn for ever with that kiss.
Though Hell flame 'twixt us for a screen.

Yea, even midst the blaze of stars.
That light the golden city's air,
My face shall stand out weird and fair;
My voice shall reach him through Hell's bars,
Across the din of harps and prayer.

I was the daughter of a king;
And he a simple knight that bent
His knee before my sire and went
About the world, adventuring
in battle and in tournament

A simple knight he was: but none
In all the land was fair to see
Or glorious in fight as he:
There was no man beneath the sun
Could match with him in chivalry.

(Woe's me, how fierce the anguish is
Of memory and how the blue
Of his two eyes, soft shining through
The year-mists, like twin stars of bliss,
Prevails my passion to renew!

Those star-soft eyes! And too the red
Of his clear lips, that on mine eyes
Did shed the dews of Paradise
In kisses, such as stir the dead
And bid the shrouded ghost arise!)

I do remember how he told
Me first the love he bore to me:
It was one summer, when the bee
Humm'd through a burning mist of gold
And fruit flamed on the orange tree.

The day had been a day made bright
With many a noble deed of arms:
All day the trumpet's shrill alarms
Rang through the golden summer-light;
And the hush'd noontide's drowsy charms

Of sun and shade were deft and stirr'd
With grinding shock of shield and spear;
And from the banner'd gallery-tier
I looked upon the lists and- heard
The sword-play ring out loud and dear.

Queen of the tourney was I set
And watch'd the harness'd spearmen dash
Athwart the mellay and the flash
Of helmets, as the fair knights met
And the spears shiver'd in the crash.

Full many a deed of arms was done
And many a mighty man that day
Rode, meteor-like, through the array:
But over all the mellay shone
One knight's white plume; and through the fray

Rose Lautrec's war-cry, as he clave
The throng of riders and the sweep
Of his broad falchion did reap
The mail-clad knights, as some stout knave
Shears through the corn-sheaves tall and deep.

So all day long he rode the press
And all day long his stout arm held
The lists, until the curfew knell'd
And down behind the Western ness
The gold sun cover'd up his shield.

Wherefore the prize to him was given
Of that day's tourney, for that he
Unconquer'd and unfalteringly
Against the press of knights had striven.
Until the sunset kiss'd the sea.

I set the prize upon his brow—
A wreath of laurel, fairly chased
In gold and with rich emeralds graced—
And as he louted him full low,
Whilst on his uncasqued front I placed

The jewelled cirque, his eyes met mine
And from their velvet deeps there shone
So clear a fire into mine own.
That thence my warm soul drank like wine
An ecstasy till then unknown.

The evening came, a night of stars;
And from the hall, where torches stood
And lit die banquet,—in my mood
Of new sweet thought,—I raised the bars
And wander'd out into die wood.

There was the evening wind at play
Betwixt the tall stems of the treen;
And in the tender twilight sheen
The summer sweetness died away
And fainted in that heart of green.

Alone I went,—yet not alone;
For sweet thoughts held me company
And new strange impulses did flee
Through every vein; the clear stars shone.
As though the heavens loved with me.

And as I wander'd, lo! there came
A far soft sound of nearing feet
Along the woodways still and sweet
Hope soar'd within me like a flame
And my thought bounded out to meet

His step that came along the glade:
For it was Lautrec, who like me
Had stolen forth from revelry,
To seek the friendly forest shade
And have his thought for company.

A burning blush rose to my cheek;
Mine eyes sank to the earth for fear.
As though my shy sight could not bear
The glory of his gaze: too weak
My sense seem'd for the awful cheer

Of his bright visage. But he bent
His knee before me on the grass,
And as his eyes met mine (alas!
How full of sweets and dreariment
The memory is) the fire did pass

Of mutual love betwixt us twain;
Then, with a sob of fear and bliss,
Swooning, I sank in an abyss
Of senselessness, until again
He roused me with a burning kiss.

How long embraced we sat, the while
The hours fled past, I cannot tell:
We took no thought of time. The spell
Of the first love did sense beguile
And made the world invisible.

At last the white moon lifted up
The screen of clouds; and through the veil
Of linked leafage, pure and pale.
She pour'd out from her argent cup
Sapphires and pearl on hill and vale.

Then, with a sigh, from our embrace
We ceased; and in the path that led
Homeward we went, with eyes that fed
On eyes and hands that did enlace,
Like doves within one nest-place laid.

That night I slept not; for the bliss
Of that new sweetness fill'd my brain
With some strange ecstasy of pain;
The splendid passion of his kiss
Burnt on my lips and would not wane.

Thence, day by day, we met: and none
Gave heed unto the chain of gold
That link'd our lives. Our hearts grew cold
To all else breathed beneath the sun:
We loved as gods in days of old.

But one day came into the land
An ancient man, who for a sword
The carven cross of Christ the Lord
Did bear within his palsied hand.
Upon the wondering folk he pour'd

The sorcery of his speech and bade
All Christians harness them, to save
From Paynim hands the blessed grave
Wherein the Son of God was laid.
And as they hearken'd, like a wave,

The wonder of his words did course
Through every heart and every brain«
The whole land flock'd to him amain;
And every warrior sprang to horse,
And old men gripped their swords again.

Then, as a tide, all men, whose arm
Could wield a blade, rose up and bent
Their way towards the Orient;
And he, whose speech had wrought the charm,
Singing, before the great host went

And with the others, Lautrec took
His arms and rode unto the affray.
One kiss: from out the dense array
He turn'd and gave me one last look;
And the crowd carried him away.

The weary days went on and on.
Dull with the tremor of dismay.
At length, one dreary winter day.
The news came that the host had won
Jerusalem, whereas there lay

The holy tombplace of the Lord:
But many a valiant knight was laid
Low underneath the olives' shade,
Where like a sea the blood had pour'd
Of Turk and Christian, and there sway'd

The tide of battle doubtfully
Full many a day; for stout and brave
The Paynims were; and the cold grave
Took many a tall knight for his fee,
And many an one a captive slave

Among the Infidels was led,
And with the rest a slave or slain
Was Lautrec. Often and amain
Hb war-cry rang, until his head
Went down; and none saw him again.

The cruel news seem'd meaningless
To me at first; my dazèd thought
Could. not conceive the woe it brought:
But soon the full stem consciousness
Within my brain to pain was wrought.

Like some curst drug, the full despair
Of love laid waste and life grown death
Coursed through each vein: the very breath
Of life seem'd burnt out of my air,
And hope lay down to die with faith.

The careless gossip of the court,
The foolish wonder of the folk.
That knew not what a thunderstroke
Had stunn'd me, of my mind fell short;
For in that moment my heart broke.

Some sinew crack'd within my brain
And life was turn'd to death for me:
A vault of iron seem'd to be
Closed round me and I strove in vain
Athwart the gloom to hear and see.

How long in death in life I lay,
I know not; for all sense was dead
And no thought throbb'd in heart or head;
But all the stress of night and day
Unheeded o'er my slumber sped.

At last some glimmer of new sense
Began to gather in my breast:
Like birds returning to their nest,
Thought struggled through the sheer suspense
That had my hand and heart opprest.

Then gradually the chains of sleep
Relax'd their iron hold of me;
And as they fell and left me free,
As 'twere from out some darkling deep
Arose the wraiths of memory.

Remembrance rose in me again,
But strangely veil'd and blunted so,
I felt no sting of mortal woe
Nor any anguish of past pain;
My life to me was as a show

Of spectral shapes, whereon I gazed
With idle eyes and knew it not:
The ancient anguish was forgot
And all the passion, that had blazed
In me, extinguished every jot.

For all to me was but a theme
For vague and aimless wondering:
My thought chased memory with dull wing
Along the mazes of a dream
Nor could it once to parley bring.

But, as I lay and ponder'd o'er
The germs of thought confusedly,
Hearing and sight came back to me
By slow degrees, as from the shore
Of some innavigable sea;

And I was 'ware that I was laid,
Corpselike, upon a gilded bier,
Midmost a chapel. Far and near,
Tall candles stood around and ray'd
Out dimly through the darkness sheer,

Like ghosts upon whose brow there shines
The phosphorescence of the dead;
And over all the walls were spread
Hangings of sable, with the signs
Of death in silver broiderèd.

My hands were cross'd upon my breast
And over me, to left and right.
Were lilies scatter'd, gold and white:
Upon my lids some cold thing prest
And yet meseem'd I had my sight

The church was void, save for the flame
And the still forms around that stood.
Shapes carven out of stone and wood.
Martyr and saint and halidame
And Christ that hung upon the Rood.

And I lay speechless and alone,
Nor could avail to lift my head
Nor loose my hands: a weight of lead
Relentless chain'd me to the stone
And something told me I was dead.

And yet the knowledge brought no pain
Unto my thought, that floated free
Upon death's dim and stirless sea;
But, as some faint and vague refrain.
It murmur'd in the ear of me.

A dull and meaningless content
Folded my spirit: in the haze
Of the unfathomable ways,
I knew not even what death meant;
I had no thought of worlds or days.

There as I lay, one after one,
The torches waned and flicker'd out;
The shadows troop'd, a motley rout,
Across the walls; then all was done
And darkness compass'd me about.

Before my face the chapel wall
Was pierced with one great graven eye
Of window, wherethorough the sky

Show'd like a purple-colour'd pall.
Strewn o'er the earth come near to die.

There was no radiance in the night,
Save of stars scatter'd far and few,
That on the mournful heaven drew
A tracery of silver light,
Like tears upon a veil of blue.

No other light was there; and yet
A presage waver'd in the air:
It seem'd as if on heaven's stair
Spirits stood waiting, star-beset.
For some weird wonder to draw near.

Withal, as there I lay a-swoon.
All gradually the air wax'd white
With some strange pallor of affright
And through the heavens the witch-pale moon

Slid slowly up into the night.

And suddenly my stone-cold feet
Throbb'd with strange burnings, as it were
A hand of flame o'er them did Cure;
Tongues of thin fire began to fleet
Along my limbs and I was ware

Of one long spear of silver light,
That stole across the glass and smote
My feet and through my body shot
Darts in hell-flame burnt fierce and white:
And still I lay and startled not

Then suddenly another ray
Slid from the shield of fire, that stood
In heaven, ruddy even as blood.
And glared on me,—and took its way,
Unhinder'd of the carven Rood,

Straight to my heart and thence did creep
Up to my face and on mine eyes
Play'd with fork'd tongues of fire, snakewise;
And then yet other rays did leap
All over me. I strove to rise.

But could not; for methought the moon
Bound me with many a silver chain.
My heartstrings throbb'd with shrillest pain;
And in the passion of my swoon.
It seem'd as if through every vein

Torrents of fire ran shrivelling
And burnt die old life out of me:
Old thoughts and instincts seem'd to be
Chased fi-om me, with remembering;
And in their stead, a surging sea

Of instincts new and new desire
Swell'd up in me: through heart and brain
A spasm of ecstatic pain
Pass'd. In that baptism of fire,
Death died, and I was born again;

But not to any human birth.
The fierce desires in me that rose
Were not of kith or kin with those
That stir in men that walk the earth,

Nor such as soul in heaven knows.

My thoughts were such as have their room
In fiendis' brain, that surge and swell
In their curst thought for aye that dwell
In flames of everlasting doom;
My heart throbb'd with the hopes of hell.

A passion of strange hunger burn'd
Within my entrails and indeed
My heart, methought, did burn and bleed
With longings tiger-like; I yearn'd
Upon some fearful thing to feed.

What I knew not as yet: but soon,
As fiercelier through heart and core
The unrelenting rays did pour
The philtres of the magic moon.
The uninformed passion tore

Its veils of doubt.—Before my sight
A kirkyard opened, where the dead
Lay with white faces, overshed
With ghostly silver of moon-light,
And from their veins the blood ran red

And stain'd the grass with stream on stream.
Then, for the vision, my tense will
Strain'd out to reach that awful rill
And kneeling 'neath that ghastly gleam,
Of human blood to drink its fill:

But could not; for my hands were bound.
And as I looked and burnt with rage
My hellish hunger to assuage,
From out the heap of dead there wound
A snake-like thread and on the page

Of moonlit stone strange signs did write
In characters of awful red;
Spells such as wake the sheeted dead
And draw the thunder through the night
And as I look'd thereon, I read.

But knew not what the import, save
That it was borne into my bought,
(How I knew not) the charm was wrought
To draw new victims to the grave,

Each with the other's heart's blood bought.

Still the moon sear'd me with her sight;
And still I strove in vain to stir;
And sterner aye and fiercelier
Desire burnt in me; till the night
Waned, and the spell waned, too, with her.

Then, as the earliest morning grey
Began to glimmer in the East,
The moon waxed paler and there ceased
Her fiery hands from me. Then day;
And mine eyes left their bloody feast.

Sleep fell on me again, such sleep
As lies upon the damnèd dead,
Who dream of horror and of dread,
What while the demons vigil keep
Till Doomsday thunder o'er their head.

But gradually, within my dream,
Another dream was born in me:
Methought God's sunshine set me free
From doom of dark and it did seem
One knelt anigh on bended knee

And gazed full sadly on my face,
With eyes star-soft, eyes that I knew,
Brimmed with full peace of heaven's hue;
Wherein big tears did stand and chase
Each other from their deeps of blue.

Some angel of the dead delight
Surely it was: yet could not I
Recall its name. Then drawing nigh.
It bent above my cheek death-white
Its breast that heaved with many a sigh.

And yet 'twas but a dream, methought.
But as the face drew near to mine,
A glow as of enchanted wine
Slid through my veins: the red lips sought
My brow and settled on my eyne:

Then on my lips like balm of fire
Descended.—Life leapt up in me
To that hot chrism: suddenly
My heart-strings sounded like a lyre

With music of a living glee.

The spell slid off from heart and brain;
The seal that lay upon my sight
Relax'd and to the morning white
My glad eyes open'd once again:
And as they drank the golden light.

Through painted pane and oriel shed,
Dazzled at first and seeing none
For the new splendours of the sun,
A great shout hurtled through my head,
As of a people, all as one.

Rejoicing in some wondrous grace.
Then, looking round, I saw a crowd
Of folk black-robed, but radiant-brow'd,
That through the chapel's resonant space
Clamour'd in triumph, long and loud.

But who knelt weeping by my bier?
Weeping for joy?—A war-worn knight,
Bronzed with die Orient heaven's light:
Eyes blue as heaven, when June shines sheer,
And hair that glitter'd, burning bright

As sheaves of summer. At his view,
Thought seized me and remembering.
Lost love came back on memory's wing:
For well of old that face I knew,
Those eyes and hair, that, ring on ring.

Like twining tendrils of the vine,
Curl'd to his shoulders. Open-eyed,
I gazed upon him, stupefied
With joy and wonderment divine;
Then suddenly "Lautrec!" I cried

(For it was he, indeed,) and threw
My arms about his neck.—The array
Of folk and all the light of day
Faded, for, with that rapture new,
Sense fail'd me and I swoon'd away.

But, through the swoon, I felt his eyes
Summon my soul back from the deep
Of death; my spirit sprang to steep
In that dear dream of Paradise

And in his arms I fell asleep.

The days are blank for me that past
Until the day when we were wed,
Like as the lightning's lurid red
Blots out the lamplight, so the blast
Of hellish doom, that on my head

Fell in that night of fate and fear,
Effaced the golden memories
Of days that lapsed like summer seas
Under the blue of heaven clear.
Blown over of the fragrant breeze.

But oh! with what a charact'ry
Of burning memories, despair,
Link'd with remorse, has stamp'd for e'er
That night's long horror upon me!
When, with my foot on heaven's stair.

Hell hurled me down the deeps of doom.
There lives no snake in nether fire
So merciless as waste desire;
No demon in hell's lurid gloom
As memory is half so dire.

Our wedding-day had come and sped.
Through happy gold of summertide,
To eve: and now the night spread wide
Her cloak of purple round the bed
Where Love and I lay side by side.

The lisp of lute-strings smitten soft,
Hymning the golden allegresse
Of wedded love, the silver stress
Of choral songs—that soar'd aloft
Till all the air was one caress

Of silken sound—had died away.
A spell of silence held the night,
Broken of nothing save the light
Rustle of leaves and breeze at play
And drip of dews from heaven's height

The nightingale upon the tree
Did with her summer-sacring note
Hallow our happiness. By rote
All that Love knows of sweet did she

Pour hourlong from her honey'd throat.

The kisses of the summer air,
Laden with spiceries of Ind,
Came floating on the flower-breathed wind:
Through the wide casement, free and fair.
The summer night upon us shined.

And in the perfect peace of sound,
The running ripples of the stream
Like harpings afar off did seem
To bear the bird-songs, as it wound
Along the meadows, all agleam

With diamonds of the dreaming stars.
That glitter'd, jewell'd in the blue
Of that sweet night of summer new:
There look'd no light from heaven's bars,
Save their soft cressets flickering through

The passion of the first delight
Of lives new-knit had swoon'd away,
And languid with Love's passion-play,
Deep in a dream of life and light.
Asleep beside me Lautrec lay.

But I, for rapture of new bliss.
Cared not to sink into the deep
Delicious lap of that sweet sleep
That follows Love, lest I should miss
Some ecstasy or leave to reap

Some delicate delights of thought,
That spring like flower-flakes of the May
From Love fulfilled and fade away,
As blossoms of the sea-foam wrought,
That melt into the sunny spray.

My eyes stirr'd not from Lautrec's face.
That lay upturned toward mine own,
As 'twere some sculptured saint of stone.
With memories of the last embrace
His rose-red mouth and forehead shone.

How fair he seem'd to me! So fair,
As I bent over him and fed
My thirsty sight on him, the dread
Of some vague misery somewhere,

Envying our fortune, in my head

Rose like the tremulous faint fear,
That in full tide of August sun
Across the scented air doth run,
Foreboding thunders drawing near
And levins ere the day be done.

And more especially my sight
Sate on the glory of his throat:
With fondling fingers did I note
The part where it was left milkwhite
And that whereon the full sun smote

And burnt its pallor golden brown.
Then, as my toying hand withdrew
The coverlet of gold and blue
From off his breast and creeping down,
Did nestle in his bosom true,

I saw—whereas the royal line
Of his fair throat met with the snow
Of the broad breast and curving slow.
Blended—a crescent purpurine.
That on the milky flesh did glow.

Like angry birth of harvest moon:
'Twas where some cruel sword had let
Well nigh the life out But I set
My lips unto it, half a-swoon
For thinking of the cruel fret

Of pain that there had throbb'd whilere.
And as I kiss'd the scarce heal'd scar,
A dim foreboding, faint and far.
Rose through my rapture, seeing there
The image of the midnight star.

A presage faint and far it was:
For no remembrance woke in me
Of that long blank of agony:
But vague thoughts over me did pass
Of doom, as on some summer sea

A swell of distant tempest heaves,
Whilst yet the azure of the sky
Shines fleckless and the sea-flowers lie
Slumbering within their folded leaves;

And yet afar the storm draws nigh.

The omens grew; and as I lay,
Meseem'd a change took everything:
The nightingale had ceased to sing;
The face of night grew cold and grey
And many a night-bird on shrill wing

Swept past the casement, with strange cries
That froze the heart in me for fear.
Across the heavens blue and clear
A veil of mist-wreaths seem'd to rise
And blot the stars with darkness sheer.

'Twas as the weaving, still and slow,
But sure as death, of some dire spell,
That over heaven and earth should swell
And gather, till all things below
Should grovel in the grasp of Hell.

The spell wax'd aye; and suddenly,
Across my stupor, I was ware
Of some new horror in the air;
The dusk was sunder'd and a sea
Of light pour'd through it everywhere.

A ghastly mimicry of noon
Flooded the sky: and full in sight.
As 'twere a shield of blood-red light,
The lurid visage of the moon
Leapt out into the affrighted night,

A shriek of horror in my throat
Rose; but no sound to my lips came.
I strove to hide me from the flame
Of the curst star, that seem'd to gloat
Upon the prey it came to claim.

But on my hands a weight of lead
Press'd and my limbs refused to stir.
Then, one by one, athwart the air.
The moon put forth her hands of dread.
Snake-like, and bound me fast to her.

A flood of fire blasted my brain:
Unceasingly the fiery dew
Of that stem spell rush'd ravening through
Conduit and artery and vein.

Till once again in me there grew

An awful birth of doom, that drove
Thought from me of all things that were
And all life has of pure and fair,
Effaced all memories of Love,
Hope and compassion and despair.

And fill'd me with a ghastly glee,
A fierce and fiendish gladsomeness,
That, in the hideous caress
Of the moon waxing momently,
Swell'd up to madness. Then the stress

Of that hell's hunger I had known
First in the chapel through my brain
Struck like a Levin. Once again
I saw the kirkyard corpse-bestrown,
With red blood running from each vein:

And with the vision, my desire
Soar'd into fury of foul lust
For bloody it seem'd as if I must
Assuage, although into hell-fire
For ever after I were thrust.

The thought of love was burnt away
By that foul passion and forgot,
Fiercelier and faster the moon shot
Upon me ray on lurid ray,
Until (but how me knoweth not).

All suddenly, my parch'd lips clave
To Lautrec's throat and in the scar.
That did its fair perfection mar,
So fiercely delved, that like a wave
The bright blood spouted, fast and far,

An arch of crimson.—Still he slept;
For over all the night were strewn
The curst enchantments of the moon:
And as the hot blood through me swept,
My sense shook off its leaden swoon

And with parch'd throat I drank my fill
Of that fell stream. Then, as I stay'd
My awful hunger, undismayed.
There rose within me higher still

That horrid gladness and there play'd

Full streams of fire through every vein.
The darkling majesty of Hell
Within my breast did surge and swell:
The infernal rapture brimm'd my brain
With ecstasy ineffable.

Each limb and nerve seem'd born anew
And every separate faculty
Retemper'd in that fiery sea:
In baptism of blood there grew
Another heart and soul in me:

The heart and spirit of a fiend.
That in all things which live and are
Seeks but God's handiwork to mar.
At dugs of death my soul was yean'd
Anew, beneath the midnight star.

I trod in thought the flaming shore
Of that unfathomable sea.
Wherein both damn'd and demons be;
Stood, crown'd with fire, upon Hell's floor
And strain'd exultant eyes to see

The damn'd folk writhing in the gloom;
Whilst, all around me, from the throng
Arose the immeasurable song
Of fiends exulting in their doom,
With hideous hymnings, loud and long.

Still the moon glared on me; and still,
O'ermastered of the fatal ray.
With lips that drain'd his life away.
Of Lautréc's blood I drank my fill;
And still immovable he lay.

But life ebb'd fast from him the while:
His face put on a livid hue
And the moon, foiling on him, drew
His features to a seeming smile,
Dreadful with death that pierced it through.

Yet I at that unholy feast
Lay, with tranced sense that heeded not
The ghastly tremors which denote
Death's drawing nigh,—till the moon ceased

And faded from me, mote by mote.

The vanward banners of the dawn
Dappled the Eastward. In the sky
A thin grey line of light grew high;
And gradually all the dark was drawn
Together, as the stars did die

And night left heaven to the day.
Then, as on me the earliest stroke
Of sun athwart the casement broke.
The hellish sorcery drew away
From off my spirit and I woke

Unto my doom: and as my sight
Drank in that scene of death and dread
And the corpse lying on the bed,
Life faded out from me forthright
And dead I lay by Lautrec dead.

No more I knew, until the moon
Roused me once more within the bier.
Since then, each night, when she shines clear.
My body from the chill corpse-swoon
Startles and in the moonlight sheer.

Across the sleeping earth I go,
Seeking anew to sate my thirst
Upon fresh victims, as at first:
So, till the Judgment-trumpets blow.
To roam the night I am accurst.

But lo! the shinmier in the sky!
She comes, the Queen of night and hell!
The grave-grip looses me; the spell
Of death is slackening. Full and high
She grows. Ah, there her first rays fell

Across the painted window-pane!
And see, her stem face surges slow
And fills the chapel with its glow:
Onward it creeps, onward amain.
Till on my tomb its full tides flow.

Ah, there at last full on mine eyes
The thaumaturgic splendours shone.
Across the crannies of the stone!
All hail, my mistress! I arise

And in my grave-clothes stand alone.

Then, as the white hermetic fire
Streams in my veins, portal and wall
Before my rushing footsteps fall
And ravening with red desire,
I scatter death in hut and hall.

THE MASQUE OF SHADOWS

Piled earth above my head did lie.
And from my sight the flower-blue sky
Was hidden by a waste of stone;
And I in earth was left alone,
To search the secrets of the tomb.
Waste night was there and speechless gloom,
And I thought not nor wondered
Nor groped into the dusk with dread;
For Death had crown'd me with a crown
Of Lethe-weeds, that bound me down
In opiate trances. In a swoon
Of death I lay, wherein the moon
Seem'd spread above me like a flower,
That glitters in the midnight hour
Above the glass of some strange lake.
And from it falling dews did slake
My yearning for the coming things.
Meseem'd my soul had lost its wings
And could not lift itself away
From out that prison-place of clay.
Strange peace possess'd me and content;
Meseem'd the springs of wonderment
And fear were lapsed from me with death.
And with the 'scape of earthly breath
Desire was dead of heart and brain.
The memories of joy and pain
Had in the life that goes before
The change of being, at the core
Of that great darkness, glimmer'd yet,
In characters of silver set
Against the gloom; bat in my breast
Their scroll-work was a palimpsest
Whereon no writing, bright or dark.
Did burn. My soul their forms did mark.
As one that looks upon a masque

With absent eyes, too dull to ask
Of what these shadows told and whom:
Death fill'd me so, there was no room
For aught that unto life pertain'd.

And so. the ages came and waned
(Meseem'd) and in a sleep of sound
And sight, I lay within the ground,
Lapt in a trance of senselessness.
So hard the stillness seem'd to press
Upon me, that methought I sank,
Athwart the centre black and dank,
A fathom deep with every age.
Passing strange seas that still did rage
In silence; caverns in the rock.
Wherein pent gases for the shock
Of earthquakes lay engamer'd up;
Red fires, that boil'd within a cup
Of adamant, and grisly shapes,
That mopp'dand mow'd like devils' apes
As I sank past them, like a stone
That to the deepest deeps is thrown
Of some dull ocean. Here the ground
Shook with the phantom of a sound,
As if some cataract of flame
Roar'd down the channels without name
That tunnel all the middle world:
And here strange midworld thunders hurl'd
And echo'd, beating back the sound
With livid jets of light, that wound
And leapt and crawl'd, like hell-fire snakes
A-pastime. Now I pass'd grim lakes,
Whereon a silence horrible
Did brood, and from the darkness fell
Into the pool great gouts of blood
And redden'd all the grisly flood
With lurid flakes. And then again
I fell and fell, athwart a rain
(Methought) of stars, that long had lost,
For some old sin, the glittering ghost
That lit their orbits,—white and pale,
Prick'd out against the grave-grey veil
Of the stem darkness, like a flight
Of moths against an Autumn night.
Spectral and sad. And now a roar
Qi hollow-moaning torrents tore
The ghastly calm, and white wild waves
Rent up the crannied midworld caves

About me: and I saw afar
A phosphorescence like a star
Floating above the grey abyss
Of waters, as a soul that is
Doom'd to dim wanderings o'er the sea
Of some unterm'd eternity.
And as I sank, I felt the throng
Of waves beneath me, and along
The lightless caverns I was borne
Betwixt harsh flaming rocks, betorn
With clash of waves and billows' war.
Toward the ever fleeting star.
Set in its mystic veils of gloom.

Roars rent the earth in all her womb.
As, bearing me, the torrent fled
Past all the seats of quick and dead
In the red centre; and the core
Of the huge mountains, that upbore
The pinnacles of heaven, groan'd
With the fierce pain: the black rocks moan'd
And all the deeps cried out for rage
And terror. Still, for many an age,
Methought the stream fell evermore,
And I with it, athwart the roar
Of Hashing powers, — and still the light
Fled farther through the hideous night,
Above the grisly torrent-flow
And the rock-cataracts. And so.
For centuries I fell and fell
Past all the flaming mouths of hell,
Until at last meseem'd the spell
Of sleep that bound me stronger grew,
As 'twere grim hands of darkness drew
Curtains of bronze about my sense;
And all the shadow waxed so dense.
That sight and hearing utterly
Were for a time bereft from me,
And I was soulless for a space.

Then suddenly the swart embrace
Of night was slack'd and all the chains
Of blackness loosed me. So, with pains
Unutterable, sense tore back
Into my brain and with the rack,
I felt that I had ceased to fall.
Then, gazing up through shroud and pall,
I saw the coffin-lid had grown

Translucent as the silver stone
That moulds the flanges of the moon:
And through the lid, a light was strewn
Upon my face, such as is shed
From many a body of the dead.
Night-raised beneath the starless sky
For curséd witchcraft. And as I
Strove tow'rd the glimmer, I was ware
That all the bands that bound me there
Had loosed my limbs and every sense
Was free from thrall: the cerements
Slid off, as mists fall from the day.
And up I stood, a phantom grey
And awful, in the dim blue gloom.

The place was like some old god's tomb,
Built high with grisly walls and ceil'd
With a black dome-work, like a shield
Of iron bossed with ebony:
And there no thing the eye could see,
Save the gray walls and die pale light,
That seem'd as 'twere the corpse of night,
Rotted to phosphorescency:
But, as I paced it endlessly
About the dismal place, that shone
With that strange glitter,—blue and wan
With my long tomb-sleep,—there was shown
To me a postern in the stone.
Built low within the wall to mock
A slit tomb-opening in the rock
Deep hewn. I push'd the portal through,
And as I strove, the glimmer grew
From out the darkness concentrate
Into blue globes of fire and fate
And on the lintel in the gloom
Did grave strange signs of awe and doom,
In unknown mystic tongues that write
Runes in the bowels of the night

The postern open'd, and I past
Into a place all weird and ghast
With one eternal emptiness:
There was no living thing to bless
The grim dead waste of that sad scape
With any sign of life or shape.
Wave after wave, like a pale sea
Fix'd by some fearful sorcery
To semblant earth, the grey waste spread.

As limitless as to the dead
The death-swoon seems, within a shroud
Of silentness. Above, a cloud
Of vapours, twisted as it were
By winds long died out of the air,
Hung like an imminence of doom:
One felt that never on that gloom
Had Heav'n's breath fallen nor to all
Eternity should ever fall.

Then was my spirit sore dismay'd
By that weird voidness, all outlaid
Before me, like a dead world's ghost;
And back I turn'd me, having lost
All wish for going and desire,
Save in the grave to rest from fire
And imminence of mystery.
But, as I groped about to see
The backward way, behold, the door
Was disappeared, and there no more
Was any opening in the grey
Of the grim rampire. Then away
Out of my soul the dull fear past.
And with swift steps into the vast
Grey lapses of the plain I went:
And as I sped, my thought was blent
With a strange lightness of desire.
That seem'd to draw me ever nigher
To some completion of my spright
Wings fail'd me not: I was so light
Of going that I seem'd to float
Upon the greyness, like a boat
Of mid-air souls, that in the night
Is borne upon the waves of light
That ripple round the trancé moon.

About me lay the night, aswoon
With second death, so still it was,—
Save now and then a mote would pass
Of strange-hued light, and in the mote
Meseem'd pale presences did float
Of unknown essence. Blue and weird.
They rose on me and disappear'd
Into the dusk, and suddenly
I was aware that I did flee
In a blue vapour, luminous
With my soul's glimmer, like to those
That fleeted past me. On and on

I flitted through the darkness wan;
And ever thicker swarm'd the motes,
Like to some shining mist that floats
Above a marish,—and anon,
Meseem'd some phantom brightlier shone
A second's space, as it drew nigh
Some other flame, and momently
The twain went, circling round and round
Each other, o'er the grisly ground,
Striving, it seem'd, to meet; but ever
Some viewless hand their loves did sever.
And with a shock of rent desires,
They leapt asunder. Then tall spires
Of flaming bronze rose zenith-high
Upon the marges of the sky.
And round the flames I saw grey things
That hover'd on their filmy wings
About the turrets, circle-wise,
Striving, methought, tow'rd heav'n to rise
On the fierce flood of fire, that bore
The skyward spikes, but evermore
The frail wings fail'd them, scorch'd away
By the red flame; and yet the essay
Renewing ever, from the ground
They struggled up and circled round
The pitiless spirals, but again
To be hurl'd earthward in a rain
Of passionate fire-flakes. Still I fled
Across that desert of the dead
And past the towers, that burnt aloft
Like fixt flames, till the air grew soft
With some strange melody, that rose
Out of the gloom, with close on close
Of sad and vaporous harmony:
One might not tell if it should be
The dim wild wail of sprites forlorn
Or some weird waftings, upward borne.
Of perfume from ghost-flowers of night.
So blended all its sad delight
Was with the measures of a song
And the mute harmonies that throng
And hover o'er a night-flower's cup:
And as its phrases waver'd up,
Ineffable, from out the night
And its weird silences, each light
Leant to the cadence, and across
The air, the pulse harmonious
Compell'd the ghost-motes to a maze

Of intertwisted rhythmic ways,
A measure of strange guise, wherein
The rhythms of the song were twin
With those that sleep in light and those
That in the perfumes of the rose
Throb dumbly aye, by some strange stress
Evoked from out their silentness
To vaguest life. It seem'd to me,
The sad strange dance's mystery
Involved all sorrows and all fears,
All ecstasies of hopes and tears.
And all the yearning that survives
To the grey ghosts from bygone lives
And lives to come, if such shall be,
Fore-cast by stress of memory:
A rhythm, slow and interlaced
With trails of pause, as if thought chased
A long-loved memory through a maze
Of desert passion-tangled ways,
For ever hopelessly, and ne'er
Might win to grasp the vision fair
And piteous. And as I gazed
Upon the dances, unamazed.
For voidness of a ghost's desire,
A strange faint perfume did aspire
Through all my sense, and with the scent
There came a sudden ravishment
Of dead desires, and there did seize
Upon me all old memories
And all the tyrannies of thought,
A sheaf of all life's shorn threads wrought
To some weird web of wishful pain.
The impulses, that from my brain
Had faded out with life, came back
With the old eddying whirl and rack
Of imminent longing; and the song,
Meseem'd, in all its closes long
And soft, exhaled my very soul
And all its melodies of dole
And striving, wafted through the gate
Of death,—ah, how most sublimate
And shadowy! And no less, methought.
In all the rhythm there was wrought
For me a sense of winding feet
And hands stretch'd floatingly to meet
Celestial hands,—of spiral flames
Wavering up aye toward vague aims
Of rest and spirit-peace fulfilled:

And with the passion sad and still'd
Of those weird measures, all my sense
Vibrated, like a lyre-string, tense
And shaken by a summer wind,
Until the influences did bind
My senses to a following
Of their strange rhythm and did bring
My will within some mystic spell
Of motion, potent to compel
The uncorpsed essence. So the law
Of that sad ecstasy did draw
My spright to it, and wavering,
I circled in that mystic ring
Of song and colour and perfume,
Athwart the wide, unbroken gloom.
In a still frenzy of content,
A sad harmonious ravishment
Of wan delights. It seem'd to me
The very passionless harmony
Of aspiration tow'rd the aim
My soul alive could never name.
Much less attain to, fill'd the deeps
Of my void yearning with dim sleeps
Of Autumn-colour'd seas, that lay
And sway'd above the iron grey
Of the grim ocean-bed and lull'd
The monsters there to slumber, dull'd
With melodies monotonous;
Save one stem thought, that ever was
Implacable, a snake of Fate,
In the mid-cavern deeps await
To fix its stings into my heart
And rend my being with the smart
Of its fell fangs, lashing the foam
To tempest So my spright did roam
In those song-govern'd wanderings.
And the flower-breathings from the strings
Of my stretch'd soul drew wave on wave
Of sighing music, faint and grave
As the sad ghost-light, 'mid that throng
Of glimmering presences; how long
Meknoweth not; until, meseem'd.
Upon the far sky-marge there gleam'd
A reddening glimmer and there ceased
Some dele the greyness from the east
Of that sad plain, as 'twere the gloom
Had for long dint of death become
Half phosphorescent Through the grey

The shadow-dawn came,—such a day!
There is no saddest autumn night,
Grey with the end of the grey light.
That could its pallor call to mind
It was as if a worldward wind
Brought up from sea-tombs far away
The shadow-ghost of some dead day,
Long hidden in the shrouds of years,
A day made pale with many tears
And many a memory of affright
The shadow-sun rose, ashen-white,
From out the shadow-deeps below.
As 'twere a star dead long ago
And waked to ghost-life in a swoon.
Beneath the sorcery of the moon;
And as its whiteness wan and chill
Slid through the void, the air grew [still:
The mystic measures did forsake
The rhythm of the dance: there brake
The charm of scents that did compel
My spell-bound senses and there fell
A witchery of silentness
Upon the plains. Then, press on press,
A mist of dreams rose wavering
Out of the earth, and everything
Changed aspect. All the waste did take
The semblance of a shadowy lake,
With shores of marish, set with reeds
And armies of grey-flowering weeds.
Across the dull unmirroring face
Of the sad flood did interlace
A countless multitude of flowers.
As colourless as winter hours:
Great flaccid irises, that erst,
(I dreamed), in life's long summery burst
Had flamed with many a bell of blue,
Mocking the August-tided hue
Of the sweet sky, or sweltered up
From the clear lake with many a cup
Of pers and inde imperial,
But now were grey and hueless all,
Phantoms in that phantasmal air
Of bygone sweets: and too were there
Strange pallid lilies, sad and wide,
Streak'd with dull flakes of grey and pied
With ghosts of many long-dead hues:
And from the flowers accursèd dews
Streamed up in mists towards the light.

And as I gazed, their scent did smite
Upon my sense and I was ware
That those curst bells the phantoms were
Of the rich summer-tide of flowers.
That, in its golden-threaded hours,
The passion of my soul pour'd out
From its fresh song-spring. Past a doubt
I knew the blossoms of my Spring
And the rich summer's flowering
Of gold and azure, ay, no less.
The autumn's blaze of restlessness
And the dim winter's flowers of snow,—
And all my heart did overflow
With bitterness, to see even these
Lie in the hueless shadow-peace.
Dead and ghost-pale: for I had long
Gladden'd myself, that this my song
Should never die, but 'mid the death,
Day after day, that cumbereth
The fine-strung soul, had comforted
My failing hope with the sweet thought,
(When this my hopelessness was sped,)
That these my flowers, that I had wrought
With pain and urgence of duresse.
Should bloom unsullied from the press
Of world-worn lives and spare for aye
My purest part from Time's decay.

Full long and sadly did I gaze
Upon them with a drear amaze;
For with remembrance had return'd
The pangs of all the years I burn'd
Toward an unattainèd goal,
Receding ever,—till my soul
Was stirred by a new wonderment
And from my sense the ghostly scent
Before a fresh impress did flee:
For there was wroughten suddenly
A new enchantment from the veils
Of the drawn mists and all the sails
Veer'd thither of my soul. About
The marish-borders started out
A maze of buildings of a dream;
Ranges of steads, that all did gleam
With white fantastic porticoes;
High temples, with pale ghostly shows
Of colonnades and peristyles,

Prolonged and join'd for unknown miles,
In maddening endless countlessness.
Grey cloister did on cloister press,
Far stretching on through devious ways
Into the intermittent haze
That closed the distance. Through the veil
Of mists, thin pinnacles did scale
The midmost heaven with mazy spires,
Round which, like ways of men's desires.
The cloisters strove toward the sky.
It seem'd one vast infinity
Of netted ways, most desolate
And awful in their silent state.
Their shadeless symmetry of white:
For, of a verity, one might
Throughout their solemn mystery
Wander a long eternity
And never come to find the end.
Whereto the devious ways did tend
In their dim silence-folded heart.

Then, as I stood a space apart,
No little wondering, from the lake
The mists that hover'd up did take
In the dawn-glimmer shadow-shape
And in pale semblances did drape
Their shimmery essence. All the air
Was full of ghosts, that down the stair
Of the pale light troop'd from the shore
And the curst marish to the core
Of the unending shadow-town.
Throng after throng they lighted down.
And in grey hosts funereal,
Dispersed in every cloister'd hall.
They flitted through the endless aisles
Of those void mazes, — miles on miles.
Wandering as 'twere with hopeless eyes
And outstretched eager hands, mere sighs
Of yearning tow'rd some darling thing,
For which even death could never bring
The death of longing: and meseem'd
Each of the shadowy folk, that streamed
Along the cloisters, 'twixt the walls
Of mist, had, in the shadow-halls
Of the dead dreams, been known of me.
Methought, in each some fragrancy
Of my own unfulfill'd desire
Was prison'd,—and with straining hands,

I strove toward them: but the bands
Of some stem Fate did bind my will
And held me solitary still.
But, as I stood and wept for pain
Of my void yearning, o'er the plain
Of weeds and flowers, a low chill breeze
Rose mutely and on me did seize
With all its fluttering hands of wind:
So that my semblance, all entwined
With airy pinions, it did raise
And waft across the still lake-ways.
Like some thin down of daffodil
Or windflower ravish'd up, until
It set me in the midmost court
Of the vast halls, wherefrom, athwart
The stillness, all the soundless ways
Fill'd the grey vistas with a maze
Of column'd arches. Then the breeze
Ceased softly from the misted leas.
And in void wonder I remained
Awhile, in a strange calm, enchain'd
By some vague sense of coming Fate,
Mute in the centre court I sate
And watch'd with absent eyes the flights
Of that pale crowd of eager sprights
Athwart the desert columnings:
And now and then, from unseen strings
And pipes, soft sighs exanimate
Of music made the air vibrate
With vaporous rhythms and there fell
The harmonies ineffable
Of spirit-psalms upon my ear.

And so, through many a lapsing year,
Meseem'd, I sat nor cared arise.
Until betwixt those songful sighs
There swell'd upon my ghostly sense
A breath of mystic ravishments.
Such as had waved about my thought,
When in the worldly life I wrought
My wish to palaces of dreams,
Sun-gilded by no earthly beams.
In visions sweet and intricate.
It seem'd as if some flower of fate,
For this my secret set apart,
Breathed out to me its inmost heart
In trails of perfume, to express
My unform'd longing,—with such stress

Of sympathy it seem'd to speak
To me. And as I turn'd to seek
The mystic power, that did fulfil
My wish with perfume,—on the sill
Of a low arch, through which a scape
Of aisles began, I saw a shape,
Array'd in star-prick'd robes of mist,
Soft sapphire and pale amethyst
And every tender mystic hue
Of emblem'd sadness, and I knew
A white dream-haunted face and eyes
Brimm'd with blue shadowy memories,
A sad sweet mouth, that had alone
In the dim vision-ways been shown
To my desire. It was, meseem'd,
The perfectness of all I dream'd,
The gathering from strife and storm
Of all my lost ones, in the form
Of a fair woman-ghost revealed.
And as I gazed on her, eye-seal'd
With ravishment, the fair shape came
Toward me, like a mingled flame
Of white and blue, till I could see
Her ghostly beauty perfectly.
There was a light of dim dead grace,
A wild waste beauty in her face.
That told of very tender love
In that sweet world that is above
Our place of shadows,—love and grief
Bounden together in one sheaf
By Death in his pale harvesting.
In her, dead Love had taken wing
Out of the ruins of the past,
A sky-pure thing, that all had cast
Its chrysalis in the grave-hush.

Then, at her sight, my soul did rush
To her embraces, as assured
In her the weakness should be cured
Of its uncompassèd desire;
But she, like a pale lambent fire
Borne by the wind across the glass
Of some still marish-pool, did pass
Out of my reach, within the throat
Of the grey portal, and did float
Along the cloisters tremulously.
Beckoning with backward hand to me
To follow. Then did I ensue

The steps of that fair spirit, through
A maze of many palaces,
Builded, it seem'd, with mockeries
Of gold and jewels, that had long
Lost their glad soul of light among
The cypress-ways of death,—through balls
Of cunning fretwork, where the walls
Were hung with arras, that of old
Had glow'd with blazon'd pearl and gold
And all sweet colours that one sees
In the fair dream-embroideries.
Wrought by no earthly skill to sheen
And shape of beauty that has been,
Fair histories of heroic times
Gone by and tales from poets' rhymes;
But now, alas! the radiant spright
Had from the webwork taken flight
And of their braveries was left
Only a grey and filmy weft
Of shadowy outlines, toss'd about
By the sad airs, like some still rout
Of old-world spectres. And anon,
As I went on and ever on
Betwixt the arras all wind-blown.
Pale shadows of old feasts were thrown
Across the many vistaed ways,
And banner'd pageants did blaze
And wind along the weed-weft aisles.
Anon ghost-music rose the whiles,
Rhythms of erst-glad melody,
Measures, whose soul had been of old
A summer-dream of blue and gold,
But now was paled and blanched to be
Void wails of sorrow unconsoled
And voices of a vague remorse.
And often, as upon the course
Of the fair shade, I took my way.
There started spectres from the grey
Of the pale halls and hemm'd me round
With shadow-dances. From the ground
The memories of things gone by
Aspired before me endlessly.
And all the passion of the past
Rose up around me, wan and ghast
With the long death-swoon, and did mock
My forward longing with a flock
Of jeering phantoms, mute as Fate.
In every nook the wraiths did wait

To spring upon me: from the roofs.
Thick with void ghosts of gems, grey woofs
Of worldly-worn desires did flutter
About my head and there did mutter
From all the caves of echoings
A ceaseless flight of murmurous things,
Wing'd with dead thoughts melodious.
The phantom footfalls did arouse.
As we swept on, a shadow-burst
Of my waste song-shapes, interspersed
With bleeding semblants of the souls
I had outwrought from my own doles
And joys and vestured in a part
Of flesh torn from my bleeding heart.
These all from silence started out
To life and circled me about
With an unceasing rout of ghosts:
And evermore new shadow-hosts
Grew from the mystic gloom, array'd
In trails of shadowy raiment, made
Of all my bygone hopes and fears.

And still, as I did fare, for tears
And weariness nigh past desire,
That lovely shade to me drew nigger
And with soft eyes and finger-sign
Beckon'd me on. Strange lights did shine
Through vault and cloister, and anon
A phosphorescence, blue and wan.
Shimmering across the shadow-steads,
Show'd where great giants raised their heads
Of shadow to the middle air:
And kings and heroes, very fair
And dreadful, sat in ghostly state
Upon vast thrones, stem shapes of Fate,
More awful than a man shall tell.
Majestic and immoveable.
Now on a cloister'd space we came.
Where, like pale pyramids of flame.
Strove up to heaven the shining weeds
Of all most bright and noble deeds
That men in life have dream'd to do;
And in the cloisters, stretching through
From hall to hall, on either hand.
Dim luminous semblances did stand;
And round the cornice, like a frieze.
Were shadow'd out all phantasies.
Gracious and awful, that on earth

The thought of man has given birth
Or dream-built harmony unto,
Death-paled from all their wealth of hue
And all the passion of their youth.
And as I pass'd them by, the ruth
That did possess me at their view
Took shape within me and I knew.
In all that grey and shadowy state
Of dreams and semblants etiolate,
The phantoms of the unreal sheen,
That glorifies the "Might have been."
Long did we traverse without cease
That awful maze of palaces;
And still, whene'er my soul did faint
For the sad stress of some dead plaint,
The ghost of gladness past, or, pale
With agony, desire did fail,
For all the horror of the task
And the grey terror of that masque
Of shadow-spectres, that for e'er
Did harass me with ghosts of care
And memories,—that fairest shade
The torment of my spright allay'd
With her soft shadowy azure gaze;
And still I strove along the ways
Behind her and could reach her not.

So we for endless years, methought.
Did fare, and never could I win
To fold her form my arms within;
It seem'd to me, the films of air.
That parted us, of crystal were.
As pitiless as diamond,
Forbidding me to come beyond
The line that did our lives divide.
And ever, as the ages died
And no hope came to my desire
Of its fruition, the pale fire
Of longing, that at first had seem'd
But as a flicker, burn'd and beam'd
Within my soul to such a height
Of aspirance, that with its light
My ghostly semblance, grey and wan,
Grew glorious as a star and shone
With splendour of desireful love
And all my being flamed above
The greyness of the lower air.
And that shade, too, the pale and fair,

Put on like splendour of desire
And in like brightness ever higher
Flamed up athwart the shadow-rout
And the pale cloisters, sheathed about
With fire celestial. So there past
Long centuries, until at last
My eyes were open'd from the ring
Of mine own wish and suffering
And to my new-born sight appeared,
Against the sky-rack grey and weird.
Myriads of souls, that like a fire
Burnt higher up and ever higher
Toward the troubled firmament.
And as I gazed, the air was rent
With a great singing, as it were
The resonance of a great prayer
And joy for a great ransom won;
And with the shock of it upon
The embattled air, the veils were torn
From the ceiled sky and there was borne
Upon my sense a great delight,
A flowering of awful light:
For there did pass across the heaven
A sword of flaming gold, and riven
Were all the glooms from south to north
And the great radiance burst forth
Of midmost heaven upon us all.
And from the firmament did fall
A rain of heavenly fires, that brake
The crystal walls from us and strake
The mists to splendour. Then did we
Each upon each in ecstasy
Rush in the ending of desire,
And in that sacrament of fire,
All grossness of vain hope fell off
From the pure essence and with love
And gladness purged, the perfect spright
Rose up into the realms of light,
Death and its mystery solved at last.
And so with many a song we past
Into the deepest deeps of blue,
A dual soul, that like a dew
Dissolved into the eternity
That rounds all being like a sea.

The Masque of Shadows & Other Poems (1870)
Intaglios; Sonnets (1871)
Songs of Life and Death (1872)
Lautrec: A Poem (1878)
The Poems of François Villon (1878)
New Poems (1880)
The Book of the Thousand Nights and One Night (1882–4) A translation in nine volumes
Tales from the Arabic (1884)
The Novels of Matteo Bandello, Bishop of Agen (1890) A translation in six volumes
The Decameron by Giovanni Boccaccio (1886) A translation in three volumes
Alaeddin and the Enchanted Lamp; Zein Ul Asnam and The King of the Jinn: (1889) editor and translator
The Persian Letters of Montesquieu (1897) Translator
The Quatrains of Omar Kheyyam of Nisahpour (1898)
Poems of Master François Villon of Paris (1900)
The Poems of Hafiz (1901) A translation in three volumes
Oriental Tales: The Book of the Thousand Nights and One Night (1901) A translation in fifteen volumes
The Descent of the Dove & Other Poems (1902)
Poetical Works (1902) Two volumes
Stories of Boccaccio (1903)
Vigil and Vision: New Sonnets (1903)
Hamid the Luckless & Other Tales in Verse (1904)
Songs of Consolation: New Poems (1904)
Sir Winfrith & Other Poems (1905)
Selections from the Poetry of John Payne (1906) selected by Tracy and Lucy Robinson
Flowers of France: Romantic Period (1906)
Flowers of France, The Renaissance Period (1907)
The Quatrains of Ibn et Tefrid (1908, second edition 1921)
Flowers of France: The Latter Days (1913)
Flowers of France: The Classic Period (1914)
The Way of the Winepress (1920)
Nature and Her Lover (1922)
The Autobiography of John Payne of Villon Society Fame, Poet and Scholar (1926)

www.ingramcontent.com/pod-product-compliance
Lightning Source LLC
Chambersburg PA
CBHW060101050426
42448CB00011B/2575